The

Truth

About

Me

Being Courageous, Honest, Vulnerable, and Real

Gaye Berkshire Marston

Dedication

To my parents, for my roots.

To Buddy, my husband,
and to Jodi, my daughter,
for walking with me through
the challenges of relationship.
Without you two, this book would not exist.

To my grandchildren Christian, E. Gracie and
Jackson, for continuing the faith into your
generation.

To Jesus Christ, for helping me unearth my
buried treasure. You restored my wings.

"It's all about relationship."

Written with Shawn Smucker
Edited by Andi Cumbo-Floyd (andilit.com)
Cover concept by Colin Burch
Cover design by Jennie Brooks Sneddon
Cover layout by Stephanie Spino

Table of Contents

CHAPTER ONE
The Blind Spot

"Ladies and gentleman, we are beginning our descent into Dulles International Airport. Our ETA is approximately 57 minutes."

I sighed with relief. It had been a long flight from Lagos, Nigeria, where I had been training leaders and pastors for John Maxwell's Million Leader Mandate. I was on my way across the Atlantic Ocean and back to northern Virginia. I was quiet for most of the journey, decompressing after a full week, and as I approached re-entry into normal life, my mind shifted back to some nagging personal issues that had me stumped.

Though I enjoy conversation, I tend to

keep to myself on airplanes, especially during long flights. I hadn't spoken to the lady next to me for the ten hours we were in the air, but as we prepared to land, we struck up a conversation. As a Licensed Counselor and pastor, my curiosity often unearths personal information quickly. I can't remember how we got there, but the lady was telling me about her painful divorce from her physician husband. She mentioned that, for the first time in her life, she had sought help from a professional counselor.

She spoke of her healing and how highly she'd recommend her counselor and the process. I affirmed her because, after all, I believed in therapy. I'd spent years helping people as a therapist, pastor and teacher, dedicating my life to helping others find direction toward wholeness and restoration.

However, as I was speaking with her, my mind wandered back to a month prior. After 38 years in a relationship with Christ, a 35-year marriage, 26-years in ministry, 16-years in Private Practice, and 15-years as a Lead Pastor of a large church, I was painfully aware of a challenge in my life that my personal experience and professional expertise was not helping. It involved the two most important relationships in my life, two people I loved deeply: my husband and daughter. I had hit a roadblock.

Obviously, the work God began in me 38 years prior had not yet been completed. Only an arrogant person would say that one arrives at the pinnacle of spiritual maturity, complete with enough grace to coast to the finish line of a good life. Could there be an even deeper place to travel into the mystery of faith, my relationship with God, and my relationships with others? What was I missing?

As I listened to the woman on the plane, I realized that neither my professional experience and knowledge nor my personal commitment to forgiveness and prayer were producing that missing piece. Maybe God's answer was something I hadn't pursued yet – maybe I needed a carefully chosen, objective, outside human voice that would challenge me. Maybe there was something I would never be able to see without that perspective. After all, God chose Nathan to confront and challenge David's blind spot (2 Samuel 12). Maybe God's design for me was to allow another human to help me see what I couldn't see on my own.

Looking back, I can see how God was beginning to reveal clues that would not only take me deeper into the mystery of faith and His grace but also unlock a significant part of my heart that had been lying dormant for years. Things in my life were about to go to a whole new level. If God called me to be a leader in His Church, why wouldn't He require continued travel into deeper places within my own heart and greater trust in Him?

The woman on the plane and I discovered we lived in the same town, 50 miles outside Washington, DC.

"Can I have your counselor's information?" I asked.

I took the baggage claim tag out of my passport and handed the small slip of waxy paper to her. She scribbled her counselor's name and number on it. I had no idea how it would eventually change my life.

"Thank you," I said.

"Let's get together sometime," she said.

"I'd love that!" I said.

I stuck the number back into my passport and disembarked to customs. I never saw her again. I can't even remember her name.

Two months passed, life got busy, and my exchange with the woman on the plane faded. I am a helper. As a pastor and trained change-agent, I help to guide people as they navigate the struggles of life to find freedom. Receiving help for myself was not on my radar. With my expertise and experience in relationships, human behavior, and theological study, wasn't that enough to be a great leader? I went to great lengths to be self-aware and to be intentional about maintaining my integrity.

Then, all hell broke loose. When you're in a relationship with Christ that happens, right? Hell needs to break loose in us and from us – so we can be free of it. Except it is a painful process that turns you upside down and inside out.

My relationships with my husband and my daughter hit critical mass. I knew I had to find a different way to address the conflict that once again left me feeling hurt and angry. My dedication to forgiving had become stale, too!

I remembered the woman on the plane and searched my documents from the trip in hopes that I still had the counselor's information. There it was in my passport: the baggage claim tag with the counselor's name and number. I made the call.

Never underestimate the importance of asking for and receiving help. Truth is, helpers need help, too. In my counseling practice, I saw many in helping professions – nurses, pastors, caregivers, etc. – who were lacking in healthy self-care. Culture trains us to go it alone, to value self-sufficiency and self-determination. Yet, our most important advances and crucial discoveries about ourselves will always happen in relationship and community. It's how God created us to be: inter-dependent on one another.

I walked in for that first appointment, and I felt my skepticism rise. I knew how challenging it would be for a therapist to counsel a therapist. I knew how to be on her side of the desk: I knew the questions to ask, the areas to probe; I knew how to help. But did I know how to receive help? Would I be able to forgo my confidence and competence in all that I knew and be the vulnerable one?

She had the typical counselor aura: nice, earthy, gentle, firm. She talked in a no-nonsense way and communicated her guidelines with kindness. She was warm, yet I could tell she wasn't into pretenses. I couldn't imagine her wasting time with anyone who refused to fully engage in the process, yet I could tell her heartbeat was to help people find a healthier place in life.

We had a brief conversation about our profession and our educational backgrounds. I told her my reservations and explained why I was a little skeptical of the process. She nodded and asked me to tell her what had brought me to her office.

I began to explain my dilemma. I detailed how I had been hurt and the injustice done to me.

I must have been rambling as she immediately pointed out that I wasn't finishing my sentences. I had never noticed that about myself. But I wanted her to hear and understand my feelings so I tried harder. I sat back as I finished my monologue and fully expected her to validate my plight. After all, it was her job to help me come up with a plan. Professionally and intellectually, I know you can't change other people. But she could see it was subconsciously what I hoped for and wanted.

We sat in silence for a moment. And then she said something I'll never forget and didn't expect to hear.

"You are in serious denial," she said in a relatively emotionless voice. I felt my defenses go up. Those five words reactivated my attempts to convince her she was misreading the situation and me.

"Me?" I asked. "I'm in denial? I'm one of the most open-minded, non-judgmental people you will ever meet. I'm a mediator. I've dedicated my life to restoring relationships and put others before myself. I promote a message of love and human value. Can't you see how my husband's behavior is hurting me? Didn't I explain it well enough? I'm in denial?" I asked again, flabbergasted.

She nodded.

"It's difficult to hear that about yourself, isn't it?"

I didn't know what to say.

"Gaye, if you're simply here to have me

validate your experience, I can't help you. If you've come for me to affirm your methods or behavior as being the best in your situation, I can't help you. We're not going to make any meaningful progress unless we focus on you."

I recognized this stage of the counseling process. Early in, especially if the counselor is skilled, it is at this point that most people quit. The grit to do the necessary archeological dig into the blind spot is exchanged for the more comfortable avoidance and denial. The risk and personal cost is so huge that a sneaky defensive tactic takes over: attack the counselor's credibility.

That counselor just doesn't understand my situation. She's way off.

I wish she would focus on the things I want to focus on.

I've heard it hundreds of times. Human nature is so conditioned to point out what others are doing wrong that when challenged to look inward, it is rejected. The truth about me can be painful; it unearths parts of myself I don't want to see. Wanting others to change is much more appealing because it requires nothing of me. Remaining the victim is much easier than the work of healing.

I was tempted to take that route myself. But as I left that day, I made a conscious choice: *I would open my heart and mind.* I would make room for the possibility that maybe there was something I wasn't seeing about myself. I know a lot, but I don't know everything, so I committed to the process. One session revealed one of the most important things about humanity I would ever learn.

We all have a blind spot.

Scientific research has validated that we all have a literal, visual, blind spot.

A quick exercise will illustrate what I'm talking about.

> Take an unlined note card. On the left side make a dot, and on the right side make an x. Hold the card at eye level about an arm's length away, with the x on the right. Close your right eye and look directly at the x with your left eye.
>
> Notice that you can also see the dot. Focus on the x, but be aware of the

dot as you slowly bring the card toward your face. The dot will disappear, and then reappear. Try moving the card closer and farther to pinpoint exactly where this happens. Now close your left eye and look directly at the dot with your right eye. This time the x will disappear and reappear as you bring the card slowly toward your face.

The optic nerve—a bundle of nerve fibers that carries messages from your eye to your brain—passes through one spot on the light-sensitive lining, or retina, of your eye. In this spot, your eye's retina has no light receptors.

There is literally a place your eye cannot see because light is not there. Think about that. You can't see it, but something is in the darkness! Just like when changing lanes in a car, a blind spot can cause a bad accident. It needs to be considered. You cannot always trust what only your eye can see.

Likewise, we all have an emotional blind spot. There are situations in our lives that we think we have figured out, relationships we think we have nailed down. Could it be that whatever is in our blind spots actively influences how we navigate our lives and relationships?

My counselor was introducing me to my blind spot.

At this point during counseling, it is tempting to make excuses and back out of the challenge. At this point, most people shake their heads and deny they could be missing something. I've seen it with church people when challenged to grow spiritually and with those in counseling when challenged to grow emotionally.

When we don't like what's being said, when we don't appreciate a different perspective about ourselves, we make excuses, blame others, get offended or angry, and cut and run. But what we can never cut and run from is our blind spot. Oh, we'll show up in a new place or new relationship but inevitably continue the same cycle. Sadly, we also eliminate any hope of personal freedom and healthier relationships through a deeper heart and mind transformation.

In the days following those first counseling sessions, I thought about what she had said to me, that I was in denial. *I considered the possibility* that I had a blind spot. It would take some serious emotional work to embrace, reframe and drill down into this new place. It intrigued me that my counselor could see something about me that I was unable to see myself. So, in *submission to the Holy Spirit* and open to my counselor's guidance and challenge, I was ready. I would trust her to help me, yes; but more importantly, I trusted God to use her to help search my heart for this thing I couldn't see.

God wanted to reveal my blind spot to me. This was about to get real.

Ugh!

As I engaged this new process of relying on someone to help me identify what was in my blind spot, I focused on Psalm 139, especially verses 23 and 24.

Search me, God, and know my heart;
test me and know my anxious thoughts.
See if there is any offensive way in me,
and lead me in the way everlasting.

"Father, you created me. You have my

permission to show me what has been hiding in my blind spot."

When you sincerely invite God to search you, test you, and lead you, it is a request He will never turn down. God, my counselor, and my willingness began to shine some light into mysterious places within me. Was this the missing piece that could lead me into a deeper place with God and *a more genuine truth about me?* This was the beginning of my new freedom.

CHAPTER TWO
The Wound

I grew up in a loving, Christian home. My parents were as good as they come. I saw them consistently live out what I was taught to believe. As the first girl to arrive after three boys, I was the apple of my father's eye. My brother told me that my father always wanted a girl. He named me Gaye because of how happy he was at my arrival.

I remember my father as tall and slim with wavy blond hair. He was a hard worker, sometimes overextending himself. I can still see that carpenter's pencil stuck behind his ear as he skillfully built new houses. My favorite place was by his side, whether it was in a migrant camp ministry when I was four or on his work sites as I got older. I learned to love the smell of lumber, the complexity of blueprints and dreamed of one day becoming an architect.

I also remember him in a suit and tie taking us to church, singing with my mother and me as a trio behind a pulpit. I suspect he was a bit rebellious from his Mennonite up-bringing, wearing that tie and marrying a Methodist girl. Or maybe it was just his mischievous personality.

My cousins labeled him their favorite uncle and loved when he came into the room and brightened it up with his presence and laughter. As I grew, I could not have possibly felt more safe or secure or loved in my home with my father, mother, and three brothers watching over me.

At 15 years old, the summer before my junior year of high school, my world suddenly turned upside down.

I was away at cheerleading camp in Virginia Beach when my 6-year-old sister walked into my parents' room and found my father, cold and motionless. He was gone at 46 years of age. In hindsight, we recognized he had been losing weight, but it hadn't deterred him from his hard work. My oldest brother decided not to have an autopsy, so we never knew his exact cause of death. What a tragedy. My poor little sister. My devastated mother.

Everything changed. Everything. My mother, skilled at being a stay-at-home mom, had never done finances or worked outside the home. We had been used to a very nice lifestyle. We lived in new homes he built – he'd sell them for a profit which enabled him to provide just about whatever we wanted.

My father did not have life insurance, so my mother was left with lean finances. His passing and her situation threw her into a tailspin. She had to sell everything and move us from a beautiful home to a small apartment in Harrisonburg, VA. She found a position at Eastern Mennonite College (now Eastern Mennonite University).

By this time, two of my brothers were married and one had joined the military. It was only my mom, my young sister, and me. A single-parent home and a 3-room apartment was our new normal. As a teenager, I didn't know what else to do but carry on. An active school life was a great distraction. My mother was mourning, my brothers gone, my sister so much younger than me. No one had their eye on me as I began to cope with my new life the only way I knew how – emotionally independent and alone.

After 15 years of solid, Biblical training, after 15 years of a wonderful home experience, after fifteen years of growing up in church, I slowly began to drift away, completely unaware of my vulnerability. My newfound college friends introduced me to the party lifestyle. I never talked about losing my father, and no one ever asked. I didn't know how to grieve. I learned to live life on one plane while keeping my emotions on another. My feelings got stuffed into the darkness, skillfully creating my blind spot.

Though out of touch and unaware of those feelings residing in my blind spot, they subconsciously drove me. Unresolved and buried, they had a powerful effect over my choices and behavior. I lived for the next feel-good experience. I partied and lived an untamed life, managing to graduate from college with a degree and no direction. Then, I made one of the most impetuous decisions of my young life.

I got married.

The day after, I knew my impulsive

decision was a huge mistake. It was as if my eyes opened and my conscience kicked in a day late. What was I thinking?

I had been taught that a marriage commitment was made not only to the person you married – but also as a vow to God. That conviction emerged and rang true to me. The importance of keeping that vow became my guide. After days of tears, I chose to honor that commitment and do whatever it took to do my part to make this marriage work.

At 26, eleven years after my father died, I made a resolute decision to follow Jesus Christ. I recommitted and surrendered my life to Him with a fierce desire and determination to be the person He had designed me to be. By this time my daughter was 3, and I wanted to give her the kind of childhood I was privileged to have.

Church became a priority. I went back to graduate school for Counseling Psychology, and I believe that program gave me tools to help save my marriage. I learned how to step back and evaluate the baggage both of us had carried into it. I took personal responsibility for how I had gotten myself into each mess I was in. I called on God's power to strengthen and transform my heart. My life began to find new stability, personally and professionally. I had made great progress emotionally and spiritually.

Yet, years later, shortly before I left for that trip to Nigeria, this nagging perpetual pattern of conflict continued to repeat with my husband. In a matter of months, the intensity of that encounter spread to include my daughter, and it left me breathless. I knew I had to try something different.

"Do you feel like you properly grieved your father's passing?" my counselor asked me during one of our sessions.

"I think so," I said, trying to be open to her question. "I can talk about it without pain or regret." I said. Subconsciously, though, I don't think I wanted to go there. After all, I had been fairly successful and satisfied with how my life had gone in most areas.

"Okay," she said. "Your father died when you were young. Did you ever think about how deep that cut went, how much you lost, not only your father, but in all the years to follow? After all, you didn't have a father to walk you down the aisle when you got married. You didn't have a father there when you graduated from high school or college. Your father wasn't there to welcome your child as her grandfather. Your father hasn't walked you through life to give you his wisdom."

Her words sank into me. I began to ponder them and pray, "Search my heart, Lord."

And then, another haunting question. "Do you remember being scared?"

"No," I replied, "I don't ever remember being afraid." As I left that day, I thought, "Why wouldn't a 15-year-old girl be afraid in that situation? Where did that fear go?"

The very next day, a 16-year-old girl in our church had an automobile accident. As she was taken in for surgery, her 44-year-old father rushed to the hospital. As he entered the door, this vibrant man I held in high esteem had a heart attack and died.

When his daughter came out of surgery, she had to be told that her father was gone. She asked for a visit from me. I had always been able to put my personal self aside to help others.

Always. It's what helpers do.

I was overwhelmed.

I couldn't help but think about all she was losing – not just her father, but everything she would miss without him. She wouldn't have him to walk her down the aisle at her wedding or see her graduate from high school or college; to be a grandfather to her children; or give her any fatherly advice and wisdom.

I froze as if it was happening to me. I felt afraid, and it paralyzed me.

For the first time in years, I didn't understand what was going on inside of me. It was as if the stark similarity of this tragedy to my own gave me permission to grieve all that was unresolved in my own life.

For the first time, I couldn't help someone who called me for help. And over the next few weeks, I began to see a deeper truth about me. All these years, I had been carrying a wound in my heart, hidden in my blind spot. Each time I was hurt by someone or something, a scab would peel back with a vengeance. I began to see and feel what I had stuffed away. It didn't feel good.

My counselor, God's faithfulness, and my willingness led me to a wound lurking deep within my blind spot: a deep sense of abandonment. For a person who was known as adventurous, fearless and strong, I felt confused, weak and vulnerable.

I had no idea how deeply that sudden, life-changing event as a teenager pierced my heart and set the course for how I would interact with my world! I was too young and unequipped to know what to do. No one was there to walk me through it or give me permission to be afraid. So, I bucked up and moved on.

As I processed the magnitude of that unresolved wound, I began to see consistent patterns in my behavior that contributed to my pain. Throughout my life, I had opened up to people around me, subconsciously attempting to soothe and absolve those feelings of abandonment. I formed shallow connections. My actions only fed my hurt and anger. I trusted when it wasn't wise to trust. I created environments that helped me ignore the wound in my heart, like helping others with their wounds. And I wanted those closest to me to understand me in ways I didn't understand about myself. Though I still believe in forgiveness, it had become a repetitive tool that served to deny my own wound and fear. Deeper healing was postponed because I had learned to wait on others to change so my hurt would stop. I had relinquished the power of my life into the hands of other people.

My emotional blind spot tricked me for many reasons. I love and enjoy being alone! As the only girl and having my own space as a child, I was conditioned to enjoy alone time. I loved climbing trees, riding my bike, ice-skating by myself. But at the end of the day, I connected with my parents and brothers for dinner and time together.

Being alone wasn't my wound nor is it the same as feeling abandoned. For me, abandonment was about being alone to navigate through my pain when someone I loved hurt me. I felt isolated, blindsided, cut off, shut out, excluded because of what others did to me. Yet I responded the only way I knew how – to forgive and go on. Never learning how to identify my feelings, ultimately, I learned to be powerless and helpless. Forgiveness bought some time of peace, but it didn't go far enough to heal my deep wound.

Forgiveness is a wonderful choice, but it doesn't heal a wound in the heart.

As a pastor, my wound was activated every time someone left the church without a goodbye or including me in the decision to move on. It felt like losing family. There are plenty of legitimate reasons for leaving a church, but when people left without saying goodbye, it was devastating.

Think about it– that's what my dad did. He left me without saying goodbye.

My abandonment wound began to explain so much to me about me. It had a feeding frenzy on each of my brothers' divorces. I had no say in their decisions, yet lost so much: sisters-in-law, nieces, nephews. I learned that I was powerless over other people hurting me. No one included me in those life-changing decisions. I was only the little sister on the sidelines. It wasn't until years later I realized this consistent, continuous pattern that triggered my pain. It fed my wound and programmed my behavior, and my faithful blind spot protected the well-hidden wound.

Maybe your wound isn't abandonment. But something pierced your heart at an early age that set the course for how you interact with your world. Something painful influenced how you think and feel. Most likely, no one was there to help you through it or process it properly. A teen or child simply goes on because that's all they know to do. We learn, accept, and manage our feelings by stuffing them. Feelings of being unlovable, unimportant, insignificant, and/or left behind embed deep within our heart and mind. Our subconscious expects our wound to be healed by looking to others. If you haven't identified your underlying feelings yet, it's probably the reason for much of your hurt, anger or sadness. Relational conflict with those you love can touch on the wound and trigger your learned responses. Most likely, you haven't named it.

The heart can be devious and competent at avoiding the wound. The tender spots within us cause us to flinch and run away from situations or people that poke or prod at it. We literally build an entire life that protects that spot to keep from ever having to encounter the pain of those feelings. It becomes our blind spot. And blind spots interfere with relationships. The closest relationships we have, those we love the most have the most power to touch on it.

If you've gotten this far and you are still curious about the wound hiding inside your blind spot, if you're willing to go forward into the mystery of uncharted territory deep into your heart and mind, there is a concept that will change your life. Personal freedom is waiting. But first, you need to answer a question.

CHAPTER THREE
Do You Want to Get Well?

"Do you **really** want your life to be better? Do you want to get well?"

It's easy to get offended at someone asking you questions like that.

Who doesn't want their life to get better? Do I want to get well? DO I want to get well?

You might be surprised. It turns out there are a lot of people who don't want to get well once they learn what getting well might require of them.

Jesus asked a man that question, "Do you want to get well?" It happened in the book of John, chapter 5, when Jesus was in Jerusalem for one of the Jewish festivals. Here's how the story goes:

Some time later, Jesus went up to Jerusalem for one of the Jewish festivals. Now there is in Jerusalem near the Sheep Gate a pool, which in Aramaic is called Bethesda and which is surrounded by five covered colonnades. Here a great number of disabled people used to lie—the blind, the lame, the paralyzed. One who was there had been an invalid for thirty-eight years. When Jesus saw him lying there and learned that he had been in this condition for a long time, he asked him, "Do you want to get well?"

In those days, people didn't have the kind of hospitals we have. They didn't have modern medicine to rely on to heal them of their ailments and diseases. If someone heard that something worked medically, everyone else wanted to try it in the hope of getting better, in the hope of finding healing.

Water was considered holy. It was precious, so naturally, people believed it had special powers. The superstition of the age was that there were spirits in every body of water, so when this pool bubbled, they believed an angel was stirring the water with its wings. They believed the first one in would be healed.

> "Sir," the invalid replied, "I have no one to help me into the pool when the water is stirred. While I am trying to get in, someone else goes down ahead of me."

This man sat there for 38 years waiting for someone to help him be the first in the pool. 38 years! Think about all that happens in a life in 38 years. When Jesus asked him if he wanted to be well, it was because he wanted to see if this man had an intense desire to change from being a victim to being a person who would cooperate with his own healing. Miracles rarely fall out of the sky and hit you over the head. Miracles happen when a person is willing to cooperate with God and His ways.

Jesus asked this man to put everything he knew behind him – in essence, he was asking this man to admit to the possibility that he had a blind spot. He was seeing if this man was willing to stop making excuses, to stop placing hope in the wrong things – water, other people – and engage personally with his healing process.

> Then Jesus said to him, "Get up! Pick up your mat and walk." At once the man was cured; he picked up his mat and walked.

He did his part - he trusted.
He picked up his mat.

Maybe you've become content to remain how you are. Pushing through to success is brutal; changing is hard! But an unresolved, hidden wound and a blind spot to protect it keeps you stuck, shifts blame, and ultimately sacrifices your authentic self.

Are you willing to welcome the challenge to leave that kind of victimhood behind, to stop blaming anything or anyone else, to stop allowing your circumstances or other people to have power over the direction and success of your life?

Consider the genius of Jesus regarding justice and personal freedom. He goes beyond forgiveness to justice that brings dignity, self-respect, and wholeness.

An open mind is the first step. Are you open to seeing something about yourself you might not like? Personal transformation happens from the inside out. Will you do your part? If your answer is "yes," you are a rare one! Most people cannot. Most people see problems in other people clearly enough but are unwilling to turn that gaze on themselves.

Hidden gems reside in your blind spot. It is the space where your next phase of freedom, identity, and wholeness is being held hostage. And the archeological dig into it will be arduous and grueling, frustrating, and painful.

Do you want to get well? If so, learn to practice what Jesus meant when he said, "turn the other cheek"!

CHAPTER FOUR
A Courageous Response to Injustice

What comes to your mind when you hear the phrase, "Turn the other cheek"? Remember Jesus' words from Matthew 5?

> Jesus said, "But I tell you, do not resist an evil person. If someone strikes you on the right cheek, turn to them the other cheek also."

I know what I thought it meant: forgive over and over again.

I remembered his words to the disciples who asked him how many times they should forgive: 70 times 7.

I remembered when He said that unless we forgive, we would not be forgiven.

I had worked hard for 30 years of my life at the forgive part but had completely missed what Jesus meant in this verse. Growing up as a girl in a Christian home, I learned a compliant, passive submission. I learned to forgive all wrongs done to me. I didn't seek revenge. I prayed for my enemy and hoped for the best.

Essentially, the only thing I knew to do with my hurt was to work hard at letting it go. I would pray and forgive. The pain would subside until the next time I got hurt. This is how I learned to do life and relationships, a passive kind of love. What I didn't realize was that it was also setting me up to be used emotionally, be taken advantage of, accept put downs willfully, and allow myself to be devalued over and over. I found myself in an endless cycle of forgive, get hurt, forgive, get hurt, forgive, get hurt. Anger became my defense.

My counselor could see that part of what I was calling forgiveness was actually an open door for me to be manipulated. I couldn't see that about myself. Someone once said that your survival skills as a child can turn into emotional handicaps as an adult. I had been taught many Christian truths as a child, but there were some things that kept me trapped in this space, and my counselor spotted this in me. Many people think that if someone isn't a Christian, they can't effectively counsel or don't have much to offer. But sometimes outsiders can see things we will never see.

"Why do you think you allow yourself to be put down and walked on in these ways?" my counselor asked me at one point.

I put my face in my hands and said, "Jesus was treated poorly. He was mistreated and abused. He is my example. Why should I expect to be treated differently?"

She waited until I looked up at her. She stared hard into my eyes.

"If you're telling me you're going to allow yourself to be abused," she said quietly, "then I can't work with you."

Wow. Her words were like a splash of cold water in my face. They shook me. In a split moment, I knew this was a challenge to consider. As I got up to leave, I told her, "I'm paying you to get in my face. I'm open to whatever it is that I can't see."

35

I left and thought, *I know forgiveness is important. I know that and believe in it! But something about the way I've been forgiving isn't working.* Then, an intense question filled my head, *Then what did Jesus mean by 'turn the other cheek'?* That question led me to discover the genius of Jesus' words, His third way, and the rest of His forgiveness strategy.

I have asked seasoned Christians about this, everyone from well-known authors to pastors to spiritual directors, and no one I talked to knew about this third way of Jesus.

Here's how it works.

Someone does something we don't like. We feel angry, hurt or sad, violated. We are presented with the opportunity to respond. We know forgiveness is appropriate, but it touches on something deep within us, often unnamed. Our natural, learned response is "fight or flight." See if you can identify what you do.

Flight is a passive response. We blame, cut and run, avoid, shut down, or never deal directly with the person, situation, or problem. We hope things get better. We forgive. I learned this as a child. Forgive, pray, do good, be good, look good.

But this response stops short. We continue with the same unattended feelings and behaviors and responses until the next go-round. There's nothing about this passive, "flight" approach that resolves anything. We cry, yell, talk, or think about how the other person is wrong. We seethe with anger or remain silent, sad, depressed.

We become a doormat.

We remain a victim.

Did you know there are pay-offs for being a victim? There are. Victims get to spend time waiting for the oppressor to acknowledge what they did. Victims don't have to do anything. Victims gain the sympathy of those around them. Victims often look godly because they're not making a fuss, they're not causing a stink, they're acting like good people.

But when you choose to stay focused on the wrongs other people do, you will remain helpless and powerless. You will remain frustrated and continue to enable the bad behavior of those hurting you. You may even be seeking out that treatment without realizing it.

"Fight" is the aggressive response. If you choose this route, you'll blame, point the finger, and try to shift the focus of any conversation to what the other person did and how terrible it was. The reason Jesus said not to do it this way is because our hurt and anger turns us into the oppressor. We subconsciously do back to them what they did to us, becoming and doing the very thing we despise. We return hurt for hurt, abuse for abuse. Problem is, fighting injustice with injustice never works.

Fight or flight, the common, natural response is fear-based and makes cowards out of us. Neither resolves, restores, or heals the deep place in our heart that has been wounded. Both fight and flight will leave us paralyzed in our hurt, anger, and/or sadness. We will continue with the same behaviors expecting a different outcome next time. When, in reality, we are only sabotaging **all we truly want and need**.

Yes, choosing to forgive is the beginning of the process. But there's a further space to move into. If you simply forgive over and over again without practicing this additional step, you're like an elephant that was chained to a pole as a baby, conditioned to walk around it in a circle. When it gets older, you can remove the chain, but the grown elephant will continue in the same worn out path. Forgiveness removes the chain, but your conditioning will keep you walking around that same old pole in the same old rut with the same old patterns.

Jesus was neither passive nor aggressive when dealing with injustice. Yet, He clearly encouraged a response in the face of it. When He talked about turning the other cheek, He was offering a third way; a way that would not only heal the wound of the mistreated but also infuse personal dignity, self-worth, and self-respect. Jesus' third way serves to transform the powerless, paralyzed, stuck, and wounded into personal freedom despite the actions of oppressors. There will always be those who oppress and mistreat. Always.

In order to understand Jesus' third way, we need to understand the context of what Jesus was saying. In Ancient Jewish culture, a superior/inferior value was placed on people, like a master over his slave, a man over a woman, an adult over a child. Jesus came along with a new message that all people were of equal value. When someone was struck on the right cheek, they were being subjected to this inferior positioning. The left hand was never used to strike anyone because it was considered unclean.

So when the right cheek was struck, it was done backhanded with the right hand, clearly stating the superior/inferior positioning of the two people. The strike wasn't as much about physical violence as it was about emotional devaluing, insult, and humiliation of the "inferior" person. The insult was a form of put-down and served to mentally keep them feeling inferior and powerless, under someone else's control.

Jesus was addressing the injustice of devaluing any human.

Jesus' revolutionary message was that ***all people are of equal value*** - no one is inferior to another. So when He said, "If you've been struck on the right cheek," He was speaking to those placed in the inferior position, the one put down and humiliated; the one hurt, angry, sad.

Even the legal system in that day would find no fault with the superior person insulting an inferior person by striking them with the back of their right hand. The oppressed had no recourse. ***But Jesus, who always challenged injustice,*** *was teaching them, and us, how to respond in a way that would cause the one wronged to be transformed with dignity and self-respect in the face of injustice, insult, and humiliation. How? By empowering the one oppressed, He turned the tables.*

In that culture, the left cheek was struck with the right hand only between people who were valued as equals. So, if a person was struck backhanded on the right cheek, but then turned the left cheek to the oppressor, it sent a powerful new message. It said, "I know my value." With the simple action of turning the other cheek, the powerless/inferior person has taken initiative to redefine the relationship and force the oppressor into a moral choice. The oppressor now must decide to either escalate the injustice, clearly exposing them as an oppressor, or admit their own bad behavior. The one oppressed, the powerless victim, now levels the playing field and is no longer a victim.

By turning the cheek, the offended one is rising up to say, "I am of equal value to you. I take responsibility for how I respond and I will not allow myself to be treated poorly. I will respond with respect for you and for me."

Asserting your God-given value means responding with respect for self and for others. It restores dignity, self-respect and self-worth.

But then, we have to see and know our own value, don't we?

No one but me is responsible for my dignity and value. There will always be those who live by a superior/inferior view of people. That will never change. There will always be those who devalue others through racism, sexism, and all other "isms." But Jesus says the greatest revenge is not to be one of those people. Responding His third way infuses self-respect and self-worth.

Jesus did not doubt His own human value and dignity. When He was being humiliated and beaten by those who thought they were superior to Him, He did not cower to their distorted message or buy into believing He was inferior. Though seemingly in a position of powerlessness, He took initiative to turn the other cheek, challenging everyone to make a moral choice about Who He was and His value. The responsibility for their response was now on their shoulders.

So, how can we relate this to our own personal experience?

What action can we take to regain our personal value and dignity when we feel devalued or put down?

Forgive, yes. But continue to take initiative by responding to injustice the way Jesus calls us to respond.

Jesus challenges us to turn the other cheek.

When we turn the other cheek, we reclaim our value. But what does that look like today? Stop allowing ourselves to be backhanded on the right cheek over and over again; initiate a new response by attending to the wounds in our hearts that landed us in that inferior position.

Each of us has to take time to explore this concept and ask God to show us what the left cheek represents for each of us. Responding with fight or flight needs to be rejected. Stop pacifying yourself with assurances that "It will be okay," or, "I can take it" or remain in an endless repetitive cycle that keeps you stuck.

Christ didn't allow Himself to be abused or respond with a fearful, human, reactionary response. Turn the other cheek is a supernatural way of healing the gaping wound in our hearts.

As we learn this new response, we must remember it is grueling to change a mindset and behaviors we've had for years. God's power is crucial. He's looking for those who have a strong desire to be healed and walk in freedom. It is evidence that He is active in your life. He said, when you have been devalued, put down, hurt, wounded, or violated, turn the other cheek.

CHAPTER FIVE
Your Personalized Formula to Healing and Freedom

This path, this third way, is not for the faint of heart. It takes grit, perseverance, brutal honesty and lots of practice. When Jesus says, "Turn the other cheek!" and "Pick up your mat," He is giving instructions for transforming from seeing yourself as a victim to a person who sees yourself with value, dignity, and worth. The third way develops *self-respect and confidence.* This is who you were created to be. But that doesn't mean it's an easy path.

The following steps are for you to create your own personalized formula (PF) to help you shrink your blind spot, turn the other cheek, and soar in your spirit. Your laboratory is every opportunity of conflict you encounter when someone or something upsets you. It involves applying the following:

SEE MYSELF
FACE MYSELF
RESPOND DIFFERENTLY

Sounds simple, right?

It's not.

It's complex because it requires you to be brutally honest with yourself. The idea of seeing yourself, facing yourself, and responding differently is based on the words of Jesus:

"You will know the truth & the truth will set you free."

STEP ONE: SEE MYSELF

Step one is like beginning an archaeological dig into your heart. Have you ever seen an archaeological dig? First, an area is measured off and placed into a grid. Everything is done deliberately – no explosions, just fine, careful excavation.

This is what Step One in your Personalized Formula is like: targeted and deliberate digging into your own heart. Begin by thinking back over a recent situation or conflict with someone when you felt wronged. (THE SLAP into an inferior positioning.) The most intense was probably with a spouse, an ex-spouse, a child, an extended family member, or someone at your church or work. You are now entering the digging area! And your objective is simple: follow your feelings – they will lead you into your blind spot and teach you something new about yourself. Notice I didn't say "teach you something pleasant about yourself." Often, what we find in our blind spot is UNpleasant, difficult to accept, or embarrassing. This work is important. Keep going.

The situation you experienced as well as the feelings it brought about are clues that will begin to diffuse your blind spot. Try filling in the blanks in the following sentences:

I felt _____
(hurt, sad, angry).

When I feel _____, I tend
to _____. (fight or flight)

Most people, when confronted with a strong emotion, engage in the common, natural response of FIGHT or FLIGHT. Fight might look like protesting the injustice, attempting to change others, or get others to see what they've done wrong. Flight might look like shutting down, withdrawing, avoiding the person, severing the relationship, or running away.

Which of these are true of you?

If you can fill in these blanks honestly, it will reveal your learned response. And your learned response keeps you stuck in a cycle of anger, hurt, or sadness. The good news is anything learned can be unlearned.

Here's an example of my response and the cycle my response led to:

Me W/ SPOUSE: hurt → angry →fight
to be understood; fight to get my feelings

validated → conflict escalates and nothing changes →FORGIVE; continue life as usual until next time; hurt, angry, fight, helpless, FORGIVE AGAIN → REPEAT

Our attention naturally focuses on the injustice that person did to me. But Jesus says, "Turn the other cheek." Remember, He isn't speaking to the offender (slave master) or addressing the injustice of the wrong done. No, he is speaking to the one who was violated, devalued, humiliated, hurt, and put down. He's speaking to the recipient of injustice.

He is speaking to you.

And He is teaching us how to strategically respond to it, not by fight or flight, but a third way. The first step is to shift our focus from the offender and what they did, to identifying what is going on inside of you – your underlying, hidden feelings.

That is step one: See Myself. Identify the truth of my natural response. Now let's move to Step Two.

STEP TWO: FACE MYSELF

Step Two is all about cracking the code and digging deeper. As you work through Step One, you'll easily identify the most immediate feelings of anger, hurt, and sadness. That's because they're on the surface! But there is a more active, less-easily-identified, deeper reserve of emotions stirring those to the surface. The deeper you dig into your heart, the hotter it gets – no wonder people shy away from doing this.

The goal is to identify the hidden power feelings that are causing anger, hurt, and sadness to bubble to the surface. Start by filling in these blanks:

When I feel _____ (angry, hurt, sad), I'm also feeling _____ (devalued, disrespected, unappreciated).

VICTIM FEELINGS: victim feelings can be identified by what someone did to me (betrayed me; used me; abused me; devalued

me, cut me out/off; abandoned me). What did that person do to you that left you angry, hurt, sad? Write it here:

_____

_____

_____

The focus is on the offender and the injustice. To turn the other cheek, turn your focus to what it touches on in your heart.

TURN VICTIM WORDS INTO PERSONAL FEELINGS: When I feel (betrayed, devalued, disrespected, unappreciated, used, abused, etc.)

_____

I feel (unimportant, unlovable, insignificant, abandoned) _____.

When I feel _____ (unimportant, unlovable, insignificant, abandoned), I feel _____ (worthless, unlovable, lonely).

This is the wound that has been hiding in

your blind spot. You tend to feel worthless, unimportant, unlovable, or a deep sense of loneliness. We live our life trying to make these feelings go away or get other people to validate our value. When this wound remains submerged at a subconscious place, it has the power of a slave-master over you, sabotaging your freedom, influencing your choices and behaviors, and interfering with your relationships. As you become more aware of these underlying emotions and feelings, you'll begin to recognize your wound. Ponder the following questions as you dig deeper:

What is your earliest recollection of feeling worthless, unloved, abandoned, unimportant, or unvalued?

Look back over your life. What event, situation or person pierced your heart, creating that gaping wound?

Do you remember being afraid?

Was anyone there to help you process those feelings?

Once you identify the source of this

feeling, you will see a common thread woven throughout your entire life. When conflict happens, this "power feeling" is activated. We learn to accept, manage, and live with our wound. We learn to expect help from others and long for someone to help us feel better. We attempt to get others to do for us what we haven't done for ourselves, namely love me, value me, respect me, connect with me, and never leave me. We relinquish the power of our life into the hands of others.

Then fear attaches to the wound and drives the fight or flight response. The FEAR of abandonment and loneliness drives us to connect in unhealthy ways; the FEAR of being unlovable drives me to compromise myself for cheap love; the FEAR of being worthless or insignificant drives us to do things to feel important. Fear makes us a slave (inferior) to our wound and fear subconsciously becomes our master. It controls our choices and behaviors. We spend most of our lives attempting to sooth the wound **and push the fear down,** mostly in counterproductive ways. We desperately want others to give us love, validate us, and value us. When they don't, conflict happens because we feel unloved, unimportant, and abandoned. We get angry, hurt, or sad; we get stuck. We engage in fight or flight.

Our RESPONSE TO our WOUND AND FEAR DETERMINES THE QUALITY OF our RELATIONSHIPS, which in turn influences the direction my life takes.

Jesus teaches "turn the other cheek" as a new response to injustice. The wound and fear begins to lose its power.

Knowing this, the big question becomes:

"What have I been doing to feed my wound and fear?"

If you're unsure, here is a list of choices and behaviors that feed a wound:

- Avoid it
- Deny it exists
- Close my mind to seeing myself (narcissism and self-centeredness refuse to acknowledge personal fear and wounds)
- Focus on the wrong others have done to

me

- Focus on how others need to change
- Allow feelings to guide my responses (feelings are clues to your heart, not a guiding light for response)
- Believe things would get better if violators would change
- Want others to do for me what I'm NOT doing for myself (love, value, understand)
- Believe God will take it all away without my personal effort

Brutal, huh? Do you still want to get well? Equipped with knowing yourself better, it's time to go to Step Three.

However...

Before we move on, I'd like to explain something to you about myself, something that might help you journey further into this process of turning the other cheek.

I live in two opposing worlds: the science of human behavior and my faith community. I've crisscrossed the bridge between these worlds for years and have found the partnership to converge in beautiful ways.

Yet, in the eyes of many, the two worlds seem hostile to each other. It is as though a competition exists to prove who has a corner on truth. The scientific community tends to resist the discovery of truth by faith; the church world often rejects scientifically proven tools that help us to live by God's Word. Clearly, faith without works is dead and works without faith is dead. God gives mankind the ability to research and draw accurate conclusions from science. Faith submits all things through the filter of God's Word.

Both contribute to revelations of truth.

I couldn't write this book without offering both the divine and scientific. My life has proven that only a relationship with Jesus Christ and His healing blood can reach places in a heart where human effort cannot possibly go. The availability of His promises, His comfort, and His unconditional love is constant and guaranteed as you walk through the pain of feeling and healing the long-term, deeply-rooted, hidden emotional truth about yourself.

You can, of course, forget the spiritual side and stick with proven scientific steps if you want. But then you would only experience this as a shallow self-help book that goes as deep as human limitation.

When your search combines the Divine with proven behavioral principles, you activate a dynamic partnership. When both are in cooperation, you can expect a miracle!

In parts one and two of this exercise, I hope you've depended on the Divine to help you search your heart, dig deep, and discover new things about yourself. In Part Three, it's time for you to do the work; to turn the other cheek so you can pick up your mat. Do you still want to get well?

STEP THREE: RESPOND DIFFERENTLY (OR STARVE THE WOUND)

This part will take practice, practice, practice. It does not come easy. You've spent your entire life protecting and tip-toeing around this hidden wound. But now it's time for the rubber to meet the road. ***Start by embracing every conflict*** as an opportunity to feel and identify *your consistent, underlying* power feelings. See yourself more clearly; recognize the patterns that have been feeding those wounded feelings. Next time you feel angry, sad, or hurt:

Pull out your Personalized Formula. Be brutally, emotionally honest with yourself.

Practice saying the following out loud:

"That touches on my wound and fear of being _____." (worthless; insignificant; unlovable; abandoned)

"Because I had an unmet need to feel (important, connected, significant, loved) in the past, I kept myself in an inferior position by _____."

(Some of the potential fill-in-the-blanks for that sentence are

- Allowing myself to be treated poorly just so I could feel connected
- Doing things to get others to like me so I could feel loved
- Invested in things that made me

feel important
- Did good things to make me feel like a good person
- Expecting others to validate and love me

My fear of _____ **(isolation, worthlessness, being unloved)** drove me to abandon myself; devalue myself; withhold love from myself, look to others to sooth my pain)

"Now I choose to _____."

- Own my wound.
- Feel my feelings instead of fighting or denying them.
- Refrain from making anyone responsible for my feelings.
- Honestly evaluate how I place unequal value on people, including myself.
- Value my accomplishments even if no one else does.

- Refrain from isolating myself when I feel cut out.
- Speak up for myself: Begin with "I feel (worthless, cut out, unimportant) and practice my PF rather than staying in hurt, anger, sadness.
- Practice, practice: apply my PF every time I feel hurt, angry, or sad so I can respond differently.
- Recognize/celebrate when I make progress.

By filling in these blanks, you have created your own PF. Well done! Every time you feel hurt, angry, or sad immediately apply this process. Follow your feelings into your wound; actually allow yourself to feel what you've been avoiding all these years; observe how you used to respond; choose a different **response.** Repeat and stick to this formula. It will lead you toward healing, freedom, and your authentic, God-designed identity and wholeness.

Nurture a relationship with Jesus Christ.

Know Him and listen to Him. He knows you better than anyone. He loves you, values you. You are important to Him. He will not pick up your mat for you; He will not force you to turn the other cheek – that's your part. But together, you'll be amazed at your transformation into looking more like Him!

You cannot love others, value others, or connect with others until you love, value, and respect yourself. That's the truth about you and me.

Remember, these behaviors will help you starve the wound:

- Face it.
- Attend to it.
- Identify the power feeling/ wound.
- Recognize consistent patterns throughout your life.
- Recognize how you have fed the wound (see section two).
- Realize there will always be injustice as well as people who cause pain.
- Allow feelings to be clues to what is

happening in your heart but no longer allow feelings to be your guide in your decision-making.

- Feelings are clues to your wound - not responding by feelings is your way to freedom, peace, and healing.
- Work your PF; commit to respond differently

As you practice these exercises and dig deeper into knowing yourself, when you turn the other cheek and pick up your mat, you will develop *emotional muscle memory.* Soon, you won't have to use your PF anymore – you'll act in healthier ways. Self-respect, self-worth, and self-confidence will grow, and you will make healthier connections. Humility is having an accurate view of oneself. As an advocate for your real self, you'll be able to speak up in a genuine way without hurt, anger, or sadness generating your responses.

When you take personal responsibility to do for yourself what you've wanted others to do for you, you'll begin to understand your own heart and value who God made you to be. Showing love and respect to yourself empowers you to value and respect others.

An even more exciting and empowering outcome will show up, too: you'll notice that others now have less power and control over your feelings. You'll be able to see others more clearly and not take offense so easily, realizing that what they do or say is a reflection of them, not you.

You'll be free at last from the power of an unhealed wound that has been interfering in your relationships and holding you captive.

This is what you'll discover as you work your way through these three steps. Your blind spot will shrink, and you'll have a new hope and outlook on life!

What an amazing gift.

It all starts with a decision to engage this process, to turn the other cheek.

It takes a lot of practice; you'll get frustrated and want to quit.

But you can do it.

Pick up your mat, and walk!

The Truth About Me

Acknowledgements

Thanks to my Encouragers: Cherie Adams,
Kellie Walsh, Jason Mueller, Kelly Padgett, Merle
Berkshire, Nancy James, and the entire 2017
Salem Fields Community Church staff.

To the person who was my "Nathan":
Linda LaFave.

Thanks to those who helped with my cover
concept and design:
Jennie Brooks Snedden and M. Colin Burch.

The Truth About Me

Gaye Berkshire Marston (LPC, LMFT) has been a Lead Pastor, Behavioral Health and Relationship Specialist, International Leadership Trainer, speaker, and teacher for three decades. In that time, she has heard the confidential struggles of those leading in the faith community as well as those who disregard the Christian faith. In a culture quick to spot hypocrisy, Gaye has a passion to equip Christian influencers with a hard truth that develops an authenticity for building and restoring trust. Gaye has been married to Buddy for 42 years, has a daughter Jodi, son-in-law Jason, and grandchildren, Christian, Gracie, and Jackson.

87530102R00041

Made in the USA
Columbia, SC
28 January 2018